Editor
Eric Migliaccio

Managing Editor
Ina Massler Levin, M.A.

Illustrator
Vicki Frazier

Cover Artist
Barb Lorseyedi

Art Manager
Kevin Barnes

Art Director
CJae Froshay

Imaging
Rosa C. See

Publisher
Mary D. Smith, M.S. Ed.

DEC 25

DEC 19

DEC

K-2

Author

Maria Elvira Gallardo, M.A.

Teacher Created Resources, Inc.
6421 Industry Way
Westminster, CA 92683
www.teachercreated.com
ISBN: 978-1-4206-3129-6

©2005 Teacher Created Resources, Inc.
Reprinted, 2007
Made in U.S.A.

Teacher Created Resources

The classroom teacher may reproduce copies of materials in this book for classroom use only. The reproduction of any part for an entire school or school system is strictly prohibited. No part of this publication may be transmitted, stored, or recorded in any form without written permission from the publisher.

Table of Contents

Introduction

More than ever, it is important for students to practice writing on a daily basis. Every classroom teacher knows that the key to getting students excited about writing is introducing interesting topics that are fun to write about. *December Daily Journal Writing Prompts* provides kindergarten through second grade teachers with an entire month of ready-to-use journal topics, including special holiday and seasonal topics for December. All journal topics are included in a calendar that can be easily reproduced for students. A student journal cover allows students to personalize their journal for the month.

Other useful pages that are fun include:

❖ **A Blank Calendar (pages 6 and 7)**

This can be used to meet your own classroom needs. You may want your students to come up with their own topics for the month, or it may come in handy for homework writing topics.

❖ **Word Banks (pages 40–43)**

These include commonly used vocabulary words for school, holiday, and seasonal topics. A blank word bank gives students a place to write other words they have learned throughout the month.

❖ **December Author Birthdays (page 44)**

Celebrate famous authors' birthdays or introduce an author who is new to your students. This page includes the authors' birthdays and titles of some of their most popular books.

❖ **December Historic Events (page 45)**

In the format of a time line, this page is a great reference tool for students. They will love seeing amazing events that happened in December.

❖ **December Discoveries & Inventions (page 46)**

Kindle students' curiosity about discoveries and inventions with this page. This is perfect to use for your science and social studies classes.

Motivate your students' writing by reproducing the pages in this book and making each student an individual journal. Use all the journal topics included, or pick and choose them as you please. See "Binding Ideas" on page 48 for ways to put it all together. Planning a month of writing will never be easier!

Monthly Calendar

DECE

1 The best part of December is…	**2** The best birthday I ever had was…	**3** If I were invisible, I would…	**4** I get jealous when…
9 Before I go to bed, I…	**10** For breakfast I like…	**11** I want to talk to the principal about…	**12** If I saw a U.F.O.…
17 Yesterday I…	**18** A holiday tradition my family enjoys is…	**19** Before the new year, I want to…	**20** My favorite teacher is…
25 Santa Claus is…	**26** If I had 14 brothers and sisters…	**27** I couldn't stop laughing when…	**28** If I could be anybody else, I would be…

Monthly Calendar (cont.)

M B E R

5 If I could fly	**6** When I have trouble sleeping I usually…	**7** My desk at school…	**8** Now that it's winter…
13 The worst thing I ever did was…	**14** I would love to meet…	**15** If I could travel to the snow…	**16** My favorite story is…
21 If I were my parents for a day…	**22** Most people like Christmas because…	**23** I have learned that Hanukkah is…	**24** One day while playing with my friends…
29 Kwanzaa is…	**30** One wish I have for the new year is…	**31** A gift I really want is…	**Special Topic** **Winter** Winter is a wonderful season because…

Blank Monthly Calendar

D E C E			
1	2	3	4
9	10	11	12
17	18	19	20
25	26	27	28

Blank Monthly Calendar (cont.)

M	B	E	R
5	6	7	8
13	14	15	16
21	22	23	24
29	30	31	Free Choice Topic

The best part of December is _____

_____

_____

_____

_____

_____

_____

_____

_____

_____

The best birthday I ever had was _____

_____

_____

_____

_____

_____

_____

_____

_____

If I were invisible, I would _____

_____

_____

_____

_____

_____

_____

                                       _____

                                       _____

                                       _____

I get jealous when _____

_____

_____

_____

_____

_____

_____

_____

_____

_____

If I could fly _____

_____

_____

_____

_____

_____

_____

_____

_____

_____

_____

When I have trouble sleeping, I usually

_____

_____

_____

_____

_____

_____

_____

_____

My desk at school _____

_____

_____

_____

_____

_____

_____

_____

                              _____

                              _____

                              _____

                              _____

Now that it's winter _____

_____

_____

_____

_____

_____

_____

_____

Before I go to bed, I _____

_____

_____

_____

_____

_____

_____

                                    _____

                                    _____

                                    _____

For breakfast I like _____

_____

_____

_____

_____

_____

_____

_____

_____

I want to talk to the principal about _____

_____

_____

_____

_____

_____

_____

_____

_____

If I saw a U.F.O. _____

_____

_____

_____

_____

_____

_____

_____

_____

_____

The worst thing I ever did was _____

_____

_____

_____

_____

_____

_____

_____

_____

_____

I would love to meet _____

_____

_____

_____

_____

_____

_____

_____

_____

If I could travel to the snow _____

_____

_____

_____

_____

_____

_____

_____

_____

22 ©*Teacher Created Resources, Inc.*

My favorite story is _____

_____

_____

_____

_____

_____

_____

_____

_____

Yesterday I _____

_____

_____

_____

_____

_____

_____

A holiday tradition my family enjoys is

_____

_____

_____

_____

_____

_____

_____

Before the new year, I want to _____

_____

_____

_____

_____

_____

_____

_____

_____

_____

My favorite teacher is _____

_____

_____

_____

_____

_____

_____

_____

_____

If I were my parents for a day _____

_____

_____

_____

_____

_____

_____

_____

_____

_____

_____

Most people like Christmas because

_____

_____

_____

_____

_____

_____

_____

I have learned that Hanukkah is _____

_____

_____

_____

_____

_____

_____

_____

_____

_____

One day while playing with my friends

_____

_____

_____

_____

_____

_____

_____

_____

_____

Santa Claus is _____

_____

_____

_____

_____

_____

_____

_____

_____

_____

If I had 14 brothers and sisters _____

_____

_____

_____

_____

_____

_____

_____

I couldn't stop laughing when _____

_____

_____

_____

_____

_____

_____

_____

_____

_____

If I could be anybody else, I would be

_____

_____

_____

_____

_____

_____

_____

_____

_____

Kwanzaa is _____

_____

_____

_____

_____

_____

_____

_____

_____

One wish I have for the new year is

New Year's Wishes

A gift I really want is _____

_____

_____

_____

_____

_____

_____

_____

_____

Winter is a wonderful season because

_____

_____

_____

_____

_____

_____

_____

School Word Bank

alphabet	desks	map	recess
art	eraser	markers	report card
assembly	flag	math	rules
award	folder	note	science
binder	glue	office	scissors
board	grades	paper	spelling
books	history	pencils	study
bus	homework	pens	subject
children	journal	playground	teacher
clock	lessons	principal	test
crayons	lunch	reading	write

Holiday Word Bank

── December Holidays ──

Christmas	Hanukkah	Kwanzaa
African American	dreidel	Jewish
angel	drum	latkes
bells	elf	menorah
candy cane	eve	merry
candles	faith	ornaments
carols	family	presents
celebration	gelt	reindeer
chimney	gifts	Santa Claus
culture	gingerbread	stocking
dancing	Hebrew	tree
decorations	holly	wreath

Seasonal Word Bank

blizzard	icy	snow
boots	jacket	snowball
chill	January	snowflake
December	mittens	snowman
earmuffs	red	storm
February	scarf	sweater
freezing	shovel	white
frost	skating	windy
green	sled	winter
icicle	sleigh	

My Word Bank

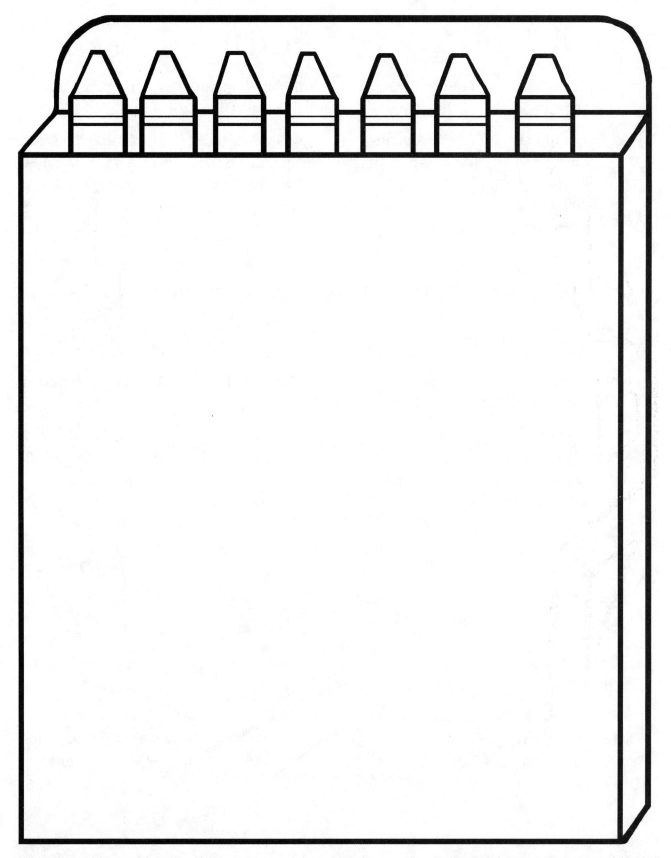

December Author Birthdays

1

Jan Brett
(b. 1949)

Hedgie's Surprise
(GP Putnam's Sons, 2000)
The Umbrella
(GP Putnam's sons, 2004)

2

Margriet Ruurs
(b. 1952)

Pacific Alphabet
(Whitecap, 2001)
Wild Babies
(Tundra, 2003)

2

William Wegman
(b. 1943)

Farm Days
(Hyperion, 1997)
Surprise Party
(Hyperion, 2000)

10

Douglas Wood
(b. 1951)

Rabbit and the Moon
(Simon & Schuster, 1998)
What Teacher's Can't Do
(Simon & Schuster, 2002)

10)

Mercer Mayer
(b. 1943)

Just a Mess
(Golden Books, 1988)
All By Myself
(Golden Books, 2001)

14

Lorna Balian
(b. 1929)

Humbug Rabbit
(Humbug Books, 1997)
Wilbur's Space Machine
(Holiday House, 1990)

16

E.B. Lewis
(b. 1956)

Talkin' About Bessie
(Orchard Books, 2002)
I Love My Hair!
(Megan Tingley, 1998)

21

Michael Berenstain
(b. 1951)

The Troll Book
(Bookthrift Co., 1982)
Baby Dinosaurs
(GT Publishing, 1997)

22

Jerry Pinkney
(b. 1939)

The Patchwork Quilt
(Dial Books, 1985)
Sam and the Tigers
(Dial Books, 1996)

24

Debra Barracca
(b. 1953)

Maxi, the Star
(Penguin USA, 1993)
A Taxi Dog Christmas
(Dial Books, 1994)

29

Tracey Campbell Pearson
(b. 1956)
Grandpa Putter and Granny Hoe
(Farrar, Straus & Grioux, 1992)
Myrtle
(Farrar, Straus & Grioux, 2004)

30

Rudyard Kipling
(1865–1936)

The Jungle Book
(HarperCollins, 1995)
Just So Stories
(HarperCollins, 1996)

December   Historic   Events

December 1, 1955
Rosa Parks, a black woman, refused to give up her bus seat to a white man in Montgomery, Alabama.

December 2, 1982
Barney C. Clark became the first recipient of a permanent artificial heart.

December 4, 1786
Franciscan Mission to the Indians was founded at Santa Barbara, California.

December 15, 1791
The first 10 amendments to the U.S. Constitution—known as the Bill of Rights—became effective.

December 16, 1773
On this date the Boston Tea Party took place. Nearly 350 chests of tea were dumped into the harbor by British patriots.

December 19, 1958
The U.S. Earth satellite Atlas transmitted the first radio voice broadcast from space—a Christmas greeting from President Eisenhower

December 21, 1913
The Pilgrims landed in Plymouth, Massachusetts.

December 22, 1956
At a zoo in Columbus, Ohio, "Colo" became the first gorilla born in captivity.

December 28, 1945
The U.S. Congress officially recognized the Pledge of Allegiance and urged its frequent recitation in America's schools.

December Discoveries and Inventions

1 **Basketball was created** by James Naismith in 1891 in Springfield, Massachusetts. He wanted to create a sport that could be played indoors during the winter months.

4 **The "shift" key was added to the typewriter** in 1878 by Remington & Sons. They unveiled the Remington 2, the first typewriter to come with the "shift" key, which allows users to switch between capital and lowercase letters.

7 **The phonograph,** invented by Thomas Edison, was first demonstrated in 1877.

9 **The first Christmas cards** were created in England in 1842.

14 **The South Pole was discovered** in 1911 by Roald Amundsen. He was joined by four companions and 52 sled dogs.

17 **Aztec Calendar Stone was discovered** in 1790. One of the wonders of the Western Hemisphere, the Aztec Calendar was found beneath the ground by workmen repairing Mexico City's Central Plaza.

Wright Brothers made first powered flight in 1903 at Kitty Hawk, North Carolina. Wilbur and Orville Wright achieved the first successful flights in a gasoline-powered flying machine.

21 **First crossword puzzle was compiled** by Arthur Wynn in 1913. It was published in a supplement to the *New York World.*

23 **The transistor was invented** in 1947 by John Bardeen, Walter Brattain, and William Shockley of Bell Laboratories. The invention of the transistor led to a revolution in communications and electronics.

26 **Radium was discovered** in 1898 by French scientists Pierre and Marie Curie. They later won the Nobel Prize for Physics for discovering the element.

December Journal

by

_____

Binding Ideas

Students will be so delighted when they see a month of their writing come together with one of the following binding ideas. You may choose to bind their journals at the beginning or end of the month, once they have already filled all of the journal topic pages. When ready to bind students' journals, have them color in their journal cover on page 47. It may be a good idea to reproduce the journal covers on hard stock paper in order to better protect the pages in the journal. Use the same hard stock paper for the back cover.

Simple Book Binding

1. Put all pages in order and staple together along the left margin.

2. Cut book-binding tape to the exact length of the book.

3. Run the center line of tape along the left side of the book and fold to cover the front left margin and the back right margin. Your book is complete!

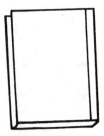

Yarn-Sewn Binding

1. Put all pages in order and hole-punch the left margin.

2. Stitch the pages together with thick yarn or ribbon.